GHOSTS
of the
GARDEN
STATE

by Lynda Lee Macken

GHOSTS OF THE GARDEN STATE

ISBN 0-9700718-2-5

All photos taken by author unless otherwise noted.

Cover designed by Jo Butz, *Graphic Design Studio*, Ligonier, PA.

Back Cover Graphic designed by Glenda Moore, *catStuff Graphics*.

Printed on recycled paper by Sheridan Books.

Cover photos: Top to bottom, left to right: *Central Railroad of NJ Terminal, Jersey City; Emlen Physick Estate, Cape May; Union Hotel, Flemington; and the First Presbyterian Church Graveyard, Cranbury.*

CONTENTS

Some New Jersey haunts post notices warning all who enter of resident spirits.

INTRODUCTION

From the Skylands to the Shoreline, New Jersey hosts its share of spirits and specters. From Revolutionary soldiers to spirits haunting elegant inns, *Ghosts of the Garden State* takes a look at the state's most famous phantoms and the places they haunt.

Why is New Jersey so haunted? Her long history and hefty population are part of the answer.

European settlers first arrived in the 1600s bearing their hopes and dreams. One of thirteen original states, New Jersey figured prominently in the American Revolution. Over 100 battles were fought on her soil and some revenants of that conflict stay behind out of a sense of duty. Others are trapped in time.

Successful business and industry titans tapped the land's natural resources and many made wild fortunes. Specters from these fortunate families stay on at their earthly abode still attached to their privileged existence.

According to experts in paranormal psychology, haunted places contain the spirits and vestiges of past dwellers. Maybe there was a fire, a shipwreck, murder, suicide, or a dirigible crash - the only explanation for the inexplicable occurrences expressed in this book is *GHOSTS!*

Do beings from beyond the grave *really* walk among the living? The report from a Rutgers University

Eagleton Institute poll among the citizenry says *"yes"* -
44% of the population believe in ghosts.

Ghostly phenomena are bewitching and
mysterious and we know little of its nature. Some
contend however that hauntings actually have some
basis in scientific fact.

As the stories in this volume attest, many times
supernatural activity occurs in places that are
undergoing physical changes such as renovations.
Parapsychological researchers allege that the physical
disturbance of a building releases psychic energy stored
within the structure. Once the energy is released it
manifests in various forms such as unexplained sounds,
vague visions, obscure aromas, indefinite touches,
inexplicable cold spots, and the incomprehensible
movement of objects.

Advances in technology have furthered the proof
of the existence of life after death. Magnetometers
measure the level of electromagnetic energy, which is
said to increase when ghosts are present, and digital
cameras can capture anomalies, such as orbs of light,
thought to be spirit energy.

Engaging and enigmatic, ghosts, and the stories
they inspire are as old as time and continue to fascinate.

Explore the past and learn about the lives of those
who have gone before us in the Garden State and who
refuse to be forgotten.

Author's Note: Addresses are provided for public places only.

RINGWOOD MANOR
Sloatsburg Road, Ringwood

Paranormal occurrences in the Ramapo region predate civilization. Native Americans revered this territory and considered the land sacred because of the supernatural anomalies they experienced there.

Glaciers left the locale rich in magnetite iron ore and the earth's magnetism could be the explanation for the inexplicable phenomena.

White settlers were attracted to the area for the natural resources that they would eventually mine and transform into iron ore, smelted in the Ringwood area as early as 1740.

Robert Erskine, who was the nation's Surveyor-General during the Revolution, managed the iron mining operation from the colonial manor house on the Ringwood Company property. Since Ringwood stood between West Point and Morristown on the military road, George Washington was a frequent visitor with Erskine to discuss military strategy.

The Ringwood Company supplied the iron to the Continental army at cost and Ringwood metal was used in the making of the great Hudson River chain.

When Erskine died in 1780, he was buried at his beloved property. Washington may even have paid for his friend's tomb.

According to legend, a brick popped out of his vault and Erskine's spirit escaped from the grave. Haunted cemeteries are really quite rare, but when all is quiet and the mists lay low, Erskine's ghost might be discerned sitting on his tombstone swinging a lantern. Some say his spirit also manifests as a ball of blue light known to follow cars on the estate's road.

In 1853, noted inventor and industrialist Peter Cooper purchased the 1807 manor together with his son-in-law Abram S. Hewitt, one-time New York City mayor. The wealthy and influential Hewitt family enlarged their summer home to its present dimensions, which includes 51 rooms, 24 fireplaces and more than 250 windows.

This American castle was vital to our nation's cultural, political, and industrial history, and in the 19th century, was considered the "second White House."

The Ringwood mines equipped the Union army with gun cartridges and mortars during the Civil War.

Descendants of runaway slaves settled in the area and were employed at the manor. One in particular known as "Jackson White" was quite the firebrand. Psychics feel his rabble-rousing wraith resides within the rambling manse; his disincarnate footsteps resonate throughout the house.

Other unexplained happenings include doors that are locked up tight the night before are found open in the morning, employees and visitors alike have witnessed a ghostly visage in an upstairs window and the apparition of Peter Cooper strolling the grounds.

Nebulous figures have been known to escort after-hours guests away from the cemetery. Chiefly, a Revolutionary War soldier's specter stands guard until visitors exit the gate.

Sarah Hewitt was the last private owner of the manor. As a young girl, she capsized her boat in the small pond on the property. A worker managed to rescue her and her friends. Her spirit can sometimes be seen floating across her namesake pond.

A visit to this historic relic is a must. The perfect time to witness the paranormal activity is right before a storm when energy levels are at their peak sparking spectral shenanigans.

Ringwood Manor used to be considered the "second White House."

LE BISTRO CAFÉ
57 Moquis Trail, Oak Ridge

Alfred T. Ringling originally owned the 19th century building that houses the present day Le Bistro Café. The circus czar made the area his home base and many of his circus cadre built homes here.

In the 1940s the restaurant was known as The Deer Tail Inn and the story goes that ghosts lodged at the vintage inn. An unknown and invisible force liked to torment the waitresses by upsetting their perfectly balanced trays - and their psyches.

One resident wraith in particular made his presence known to an Englishman who bought the building in the 1960s. The phantom, who identified himself as Armon Hirsuit, frequently appeared on the staircase and spoke to the proprietor.

No record of such a person was ever found, but it is believed that he was a long time employee who hung himself on the premises.

When a tenant in an upstairs apartment complained that *"a ghost was biting her children,"* a psychic was called in to help. The perpetrator turned out to be a woman in a blue Victorian-era dress. She claimed to be the inn's caretaker and explained that she had been there for a *very* long time.

VICTORIAN MANSION
Midland Park

Built during the Civil War, this private home is one of New Jersey's most notorious haunted houses – and frightfully so. The mansion saw more than its share of untimely death and the tragedies suffered here hung like a shroud around the house.

In 1952 psychic artist Ethelyn Woodlock and her family moved into the Victorian dwelling. After some research she ascertained that her new home was haunted and that most of the ghosts originated with the Crayhay family who lived here from 1906 to 1934.

Max Crayhay was a wealthy businessman who shot himself to death in the barn in 1911. Little is known about what drove him to suicide but his revenant remained behind haunting the downstairs hall.

The leading ghost was that of a sixteen-year-old neighborhood girl named Rose who kept a lonely vigil walking the upstairs hallway. She fell to her death while trying to climb out a window to elope with a servant who had fathered her unborn child. Her cruel and unforgiving aunt also haunted the house.

Ethelyn unconsciously painted the angry aunt's presence into one of her paintings and the sensitive artist also captured an impression of Rose in the painting's background design. The girl's countenance had deep-set eyes, bangs, golden brown hair and a small mouth.

Ethelyn tried to extricate the spirits in the house by painting tunnels on canvases and directing them to go through the burrows and over to the other side. Her suggestion was not altogether successful.

An elderly woman, thought to be a former owner, was shot and killed during a robbery in the house. Ethelyn awoke one night and saw this spirit hovering over her head. Before Ethelyn could react, the ghost bit her nose!

Woodlock opened the house for tours and literally hundreds of people were witnesses to ghostly displays.

The most frequently sighted spectral resident was a yellow and white cat who napped in a small third-floor bedroom. Wherever the cat slept, she left behind an indented warm spot on the pillow where it had lain.

Ethelyn wrote about her experiences living in the house in her book *When Dreams Have Wings*. At last report, the artist was in her nineties and residing in Florida in a haunt-free house.

STEUBEN HOUSE
1209 Main Street, River Edge

River Edge played an important role in our nation's history when in November 1776 George Washington successfully led his army over the Hackensack New Bridge to avoid a surprise attack from the British. At that time, Loyalist Jan Zabriskie owned the 1713 sandstone house perched at this strategic location.

The Zabriskie tract was an important site used by both British and Continental Armies as their military headquarters and campgrounds.

After the war, the confiscated property was presented to Major General Baron Von Steuben in gratitude for his service to the colonies. Because of his status, Steuben felt he deserved a larger endowment; nevertheless, he lived in the house for a short time, but eventually sold it back to the Zabriskie family.

The General's ghost did come back for a visit in 1951, however. A female tourist saw him sitting in a chair and he spoke to her in what seemed like a *"faraway voice"* inquiring about George Washington and the state of the union. Von Steuben seemed very surprised when told the date, and then he suddenly vanished.

There have been no further sightings. The Baron's spirit may still linger but he remains out of sight.

HOBART MANOR
Wayne

Today the building known as Hobart Manor at William Paterson University houses the offices of the college president and other administrative staff. The grand structure also hosts special events in its impeccably restored turn-of-the-century reception rooms.

Long before the manor house became the campus centerpiece, it was the country estate of John McCullough. The Scottish immigrant made a fortune in the wool industry and constructed a two-story turreted castle in 1877 when the area was a convenient getaway for Paterson's city dwellers seeking solace and recreation in the mountains.

In 1902 the widow of Garret Augustus Hobart, the twenty-fourth vice-president of the United States under William McKinley, purchased the manor house for her son. After an extensive renovation in 1915, expanding the structure to a forty-room house, the Tudor-style mansion became a high society enclave.

In 1941 both mother and son, Garret Jr., died in the house only eight months apart.

Word around campus is that the shadows of these two, and possibly others, remain at the splendid estate.

College security officials maintain that the spirit of Mrs. Hobart still walks the hallowed halls. Employees at the university who have witnessed her ghost claim that she seems to be going about the house performing her daily chores as if she was still alive.

Her apparition appears as a vague white form most often sighted on the main staircase. In life, she was a frequent hostess for festive holiday parties and important social gatherings. One can imagine the woman of this stately house alighting the stairs to greet her guests.

When the manor was totally renovated in 1985, electrical and plumbing repairs were made and the windows, marble fireplaces, and original hardwood floors restored. This revitalization may have breathed new life into Mrs. Hobart's resting spirit as well. Perhaps she is caught in an earthly loop where she replays her human role as hostess over and over again on the grand stairway.

Also, the sound of someone playing the piano is heard here in the still of the night, but please note, there is no piano in the building.

Sightings of the faces of other family members peering out the leaded glass windowpanes have been reported on occasion.

A psychic "reading" the building glimpsed the spirit of a young man sitting on the staircase reading a newspaper. Could this be Garret's ghost keeping his family members company as they continue to enjoy the elegant life of times gone by at their country estate?

The interior of the Darress Theatre as it appeared in 1919.
(Photo provided by Bruce Bertrand).

DARRESS THEATRE
615 Main Street, Boonton

If you're endowed with a keen perception you won't need a pair of 3-D viewing glasses to catch a glimpse of the ghosts floating about in this playhouse.

The Darress Theatre opened in 1919 and showcased the vaudeville acts of Edgar Bergen and Charlie McCarthy, George Burns, Abbott & Costello (both NJ natives), and Harry Houdini, to name a few.

The present owners bought and restored the failing building in 1980. The renewed theater now houses a photo shop, video and audio-recording studio, and theatergoers, both past and present, enjoy live theatre, concerts, and movies.

After hours when the clamor of the crowd has subsided, the subtle sound of disembodied voices singing and discarnate footsteps walking echo in the vacuous hall. Theater seats move on their own. Are spectral spectators enjoying a long ago spectacular?

Employees see shadowy figures in their peripheral vision near the stage and *"indistinct floating masses"* whirl about the cinema. Co-owner Tom Timbrook claims the unearthly visitors are happy to be in attendance because a feeling of peace and contentment pervades the vintage space.

Watch and you may see a phantom performance.

JIMMY'S AMERICAN GRILL
217 South Street, Morristown

For generations the Sayre family lived in this 1749 structure. In 1833, Judge Samuel Sayre made a fatal decision when he hired a West Indian sailor, Antoine Le Blanc, to work as a farmhand.

Unfamiliar with the language, Le Blanc didn't realize his pay was in room and board not wages. The proud foreigner resented the menial work and taking orders from the servant girl Phoebe. As he lay awake at night in his confined basement room he boiled with bitterness and frustration.

Eventually Le Blanc's anger exploded in a crazed frenzy and he bludgeoned the Judge, his wife, and Phoebe to death. The murderer mistakenly believed the family kept a large cache of money in the house, but when he discovered only a small sum, he frantically filled his satchels with anything valuable and fled.

During his escape, pieces of loot fell out of his bags leaving an easy trail for the authorities. They found the brazen killer close by in Mosquito Tavern at Hackensack Meadows enjoying a meal.

Le Blanc was promptly apprehended and returned to Morristown to stand trial. The case was sensational. Le Blanc was duly convicted and hanged on the village green to the town's people's satisfaction.

To pay for the criminal's prosecution and the ensuing celebration, skin peeled from Le Blanc's corpse was fashioned into wallets and purses that were sold as souvenirs. To this day, these ghoulish momentoes are still found tucked away in the dark corners of attics and dresser drawers and in the town's museum.

The Sayre house soon gained a haunted reputation, which continued when it was first turned into a restaurant in 1949. Some say the environment is imprinted with the terrified emotions endured by the victims during their bloody massacre.

Jimmy's American Grill menu offers the story of the triple murder and subsequent paranormal manifestations at the restaurant. Unexplainable phenomena such as self-opening doors, swinging chandeliers, chair rocking, and candles re-lighting themselves often occur; whispers and the sound of revelers fill empty rooms.

There is some debate as to the identity of the ghost, however.

The room that once served as Phoebe's bedroom is noticeably cold and the wait staff sometimes see a blurred female reflection in the room's mirror that is not their own!

Psychic investigators say that it is Antoine Le Blanc's dark denizen that still haunts the place and that his psychic residue lingers in the town where so many remnants of his physical remains remain.

DREW UNIVERSITY
Madison

Who's haunting the attic of the Hoyt-Browne dormitory at Drew University? Students call the invisible resident "Carol," a former student who may have committed suicide by jumping from the upper floor window. Lights appear in the attic window, yet when security checks it out, they find nobody there. What they *do* discover is that the furniture stored up there has been rearranged.

The story of Carol's untimely death and the various accounts of unusual phenomena in the building support the theory that there's an entity upstairs who could be responsible for the redecorating.

Officials at the school don't formally acknowledge the existence of ghosts roaming the vintage campus, nevertheless these stories reflect the school's history.

In another student residence, Holloway House, roommates observed glass candleholders shatter and a dark blurry form materialize on the bed.

A painting of the founder's wife, Roxanna, hangs in the lobby of Mead Hall. Some students feel that her portrait emits a haunting aura, which seems to permeate the corridors.

During a 1989 fire as the firemen were trying to rescue a woman caught in the conflagration, she vanished before their eyes! A photographer captured the image of a pallid female on film in the middle of the blaze and the photo bears a striking resemblance to Mrs. Mead.

Another ghost was reported in the Bowne Theater during a rehearsal one night. The phantom, wearing an old-fashioned gray running suit, was seen walking up the spiral staircase to the balcony. The specter grew dimmer and dimmer and dissipated before he made it to the top of the stairs. *"The balcony used to be an indoor track, so it makes sense that he would appear there,"* said one of the student witnesses.

"Reggie" is another campus ghost who is said to have drowned in the pool originally in the theater's basement. Reggie's spirit was seen walking *through* the boarded up floor to take a dive into the phantom pool. His apparition has also been observed changing clothes in what was once the men's locker room.

Castle-like S.W. Browne Hall is home to a tall dark shade who plays a phantom piano. The music lures unsuspecting listeners up the staircase, where they find *no one there.*

Another student often visited the chapel unaware of its haunted history. One night he heard the sound of breathing but no one else was in the room with him. He continued praying with more fervor, but the sensation of being watched was so intense and the breathing so loud and close and heavy that he literally raced out of the place.

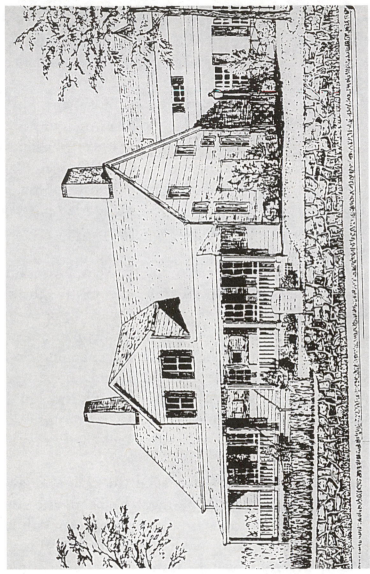

*Artist's rendering of the former Bernardsville Public Library,
2 Morristown Road. (Sketch used by permission.)*

BERNARDSVILLE PUBLIC LIBRARY
Bernardsville

The sturdy clapboard building that housed the Bernardsville Public Library for ninety-five years was originally called the Vealtown Tavern. Constructed in the 1700s, the inn was a stopover for weary travelers and the officers and ranks of the Continental Army.

During the Revolutionary War Captain John Parker owned the tavern. His daughter Phyllis was in love with Dr. Byram who was a tenant at the inn.

When valuable military documents were discovered to be missing, General "Mad" Anthony Wayne recognized the doctor as Aaron Wilde a Tory spy. Wilde was captured at Blazure's Corner, convicted from papers found in his pocket, and hanged. His lifeless body was placed in a large box and brought back to the Vealtown Tavern. They kept his death a secret from Phyllis.

Since Byram was a physician it was not unusual for him to be gone for days at a time. This time however Phyllis intuitively knew something was wrong. She had heard the men whispering and she noticed how they averted her eyes - and her questions.

In the middle of the night she crept to the box and pried the lid open. When everyone awoke to her horrific screams, they knew she had discovered the bulging eyed corpse of her beloved. When they went to console the hysterical girl, they found the dreadful shock had driven her insane.

One hundred years later on the anniversary of Byram's death, Phyllis' crazed moaning was again heard throughout the historic house. The terrified family living there at the time fled.

After 1900, when the library purchased the building, wild weeping could be heard in the original tavern room section of the library as well as muffled voices, skirts rustling, and footsteps on the stairway.

Phyllis was often sighted from outside the building by those looking in during off-hours. Police officers peering through the windows for a security check spotted a female figure in Revolutionary War era dress. When they entered the library, she couldn't be found.

After renovations in 1974, Phyllis' apparition started to be seen throughout the library's vintage rooms. In November 1989, a child saw the ghost of a woman in a long white dress in the reading room.

When the library moved to its new location in 2000, Phyllis apparently moved with them. The staff wanted to take photos of their new facilities but the camera wouldn't work. Computers left on during the lunch hour were found shut down when the workers returned - their "saved" work was lost in cyberspace.

Phyllis appears to be back. However, it is more likely that she never left.

BRANCH BROOK PARK
Clifton Avenue, Newark

Dedicated in 1895, this was the first city park in the United States. Situated on a marsh known as Old Blue Jay Swamp, the area was used as an army training camp during the Civil War. The Frederick Law Olmsted firm of Central Park fame, designed the parkland. The beaux-arts entrance gate on Lake Street was a gift from the Ballantine family famous Newark brewers.

The park is best known for its 3,000 Japanese cherry trees which, when in bloom, rival the display of those in Washington, DC.

The park is also known for a unique spectacle that occurred about twenty-five years ago.

On a dark and rainy night in 1976, a newlywed couple was being driven home from their wedding reception. As a special treat the chauffeur took them through the park. He guided the vehicle around a treacherous bend, but the car veered out of control on the wet road and slammed into a huge tree. The men survived the crash, but the young bride, still in her white wedding gown, was killed instantly.

Two weeks after the collision, there was another one at the same spot. A few weeks later, another fatal accident at the tree. Soon rumors began to spread that the stretch of road was cursed.

Another story circulated that a young couple travelling through the park had seen a woman dressed in a wedding gown by the side of the road near the tree. This began a flood of reports among locals of encounters with "The White Lady of Branch Brook Park," as she had become known.

The most chilling sighting of all, however, was the appearance of a discarnate wedding dress blowing in the wind. No arms, no legs, no head. Just a wedding dress with the sleeves outstretched slowly turning in mid-air! Where the head should be, a pair of bright green eyes stared straight ahead.

On rainy nights, a large number of accidents occurred at the tree. No wonder - the road was aligned straight toward the tree and then suddenly veered off to the right within five feet of the massive trunk. With such a hazardous turn, it was no surprise that so many casualties took place there. Eventually the road was re-routed so that it passed away from the tree line.

Some blamed the appearances of the White Lady on the mishaps, but after the road was re-routed the accidents stopped.

So did the apparitions of the White Lady and her mysterious wedding gown.

Rather then fault the White Lady, some applaud her post-mortem mission to warn passing motorists of the impending danger.

CENTRAL RAILROAD OF NJ TERMINAL
Liberty State Park, Jersey City

In the 19th and early 20th centuries, the area that is now Liberty State Park was a bustling freight and passenger transportation center. Located in the northern section of the park is the Central Railroad of New Jersey Terminal (CRRNJ).

Along with the Statue of Liberty and Ellis Island, the CRRNJ Terminal played an important role in our nation's immigration history.

Lady Liberty was first to greet the settlers from abroad. After being processed at Ellis Island 8 million immigrants purchased tickets at the terminal and boarded the trains that would take them to freedom and opportunity. The depot served as the gateway to the attainment of the newcomers' hopes and dreams of their new life in America.

Constructed in 1889 along the Hudson River, the CRRNJ Terminal is a splendid three-story building that today presents exhibits on the history of the area. In its glory days the station, reminiscent of a French chateau, was the centerpiece of New Jersey's transportation system. In 1915, about 50,000 passengers passed through the terminal each day.

*A Central Railroad of New Jersey Terminal employee weathered overnight
in the staff dormitory room and possibly has never left.*

On the third floor of the grand building there is a room that was at one time used as a dormitory. Workers who were unable to make it home because of bad weather were assured of overnight accommodations.

One summer evening in 1990, a historic preservation specialist stayed late to catch up on paperwork. Her concentration was interrupted when she heard the sound of someone walking in the former upstairs sleeping quarters. Thinking it was an errant tourist, she left her desk to escort the visitor out of the building.

"Hello, hello. The park is closed," she called out, but there was no response. The footsteps continued as she approached the dorm. She entered the room and found it empty! When she called out again, the door slammed behind her and the preservationist heard someone running away. Immediately she opened the door to make sure the intruder left, *but the sound stopped and nobody was there.*

The woman kept the happening to herself for a long time, but eventually she shared her experience with co-workers. They too confided to regularly hearing footsteps after hours and also admitted to the unnerving and persistent sensation of being watched.

Clinton's Red Mill is popular with photographers and an unseen prankster.

RED MILL
56 Main Street, Clinton

Many will recognize the most photographed location in the Garden State, the 200-year-old Red Mill situated on the banks of the South Branch of the Raritan River.

Known originally as Hunt's Mill, Clinton's showpiece has produced lamb's wool, linseed oil, talc, grist, graphite, gypsum, and corn meal. The millhouse also served as a basket-making factory supplying the county's peach growers.

Today it is part of the Hunterdon Historical Museum. The scenic site is the backdrop for some strange and unexplained phenomena.

There have been many reports of mysterious sounds in the building. In 1992, the director and curator of the mill heard the distinct clamor of a gong, which was used as a warning bell when the plant was in operation. The alarm hadn't been used for decades. The following year the clacking of keys on a manual typewriter echoed in the building, yet the nearest typewriter is in storage 1000 feet away.

A séance was conducted to identify the phantom prankster. The medium received a psychic impression that it was a child injured at the mill who was making all the racket.

The brooding Union Hotel – home to a little lost girl ghost?

UNION HOTEL
76 Main Street, Flemington

This ominous four-story brick edifice with its imposing mansard roof and gingerbread porch was considered New Jersey's finest hotel in 1878 when it boasted heat and indoor plumbing - revered luxuries.

Real notoriety came to the Union Hotel in 1935 when the Lindbergh baby kidnapping case was tried across the street at the Hunterton County Courthouse. Every niche of the hotel was crammed with journalists covering the "Trial of the Century." The bar and restaurant served patrons twenty-four hours a day.

In 1986 when the hotel underwent remodeling, the sleeping revenants residing in the historic dwelling awakened and made their displeasure known.

One terrifying event occurred after the bouncer had locked up the place for the night. He and his co-workers were shaken to the core when suddenly the hotel's heavy wooden doors blew wide open bringing in an icy wind - and who knows what else... They stared in awe as a pair of little girl's patent-leather shoes walked up the main stairway. *Just shoes – no body!*

Another time, as a waitress was carrying her cash drawer to the office, she heard a disembodied voice humming a child's lullaby. She dropped her drawer full of money and ran out of the building never to return.

HUNT HOUSE
Phillipsburg

In 1998 the *American Movie Classics Channel* filmed the introduction to their Halloween film fest at this house when the long dead live on.

"Hundreds of times" occupants of the private home have experienced the appearance of a female apparition in a dark hooded cloak. Her routine never wavers. She passes by the kitchen window and then proceeds toward the back door and vanishes. The woman is thought to be the ghost of Mary Insley Hunt.

Edward Hunt built parts of the house in 1772 but the main structure was completed in 1825 by his grandson. He died in the house in 1864 and his wife Mary lived there until her death in 1882.

The spectral phenomenon began shortly after the building was renovated in 1976. Since then the visual and auditory anomalies are too numerous to recount.

Occasionally a young boy is seen in the house and an old man ghost sits on a chair in the hallway. Footsteps are often heard and the surroundings get icy cold, *"like it always does when something is going to happen,"* said the owner.

MURPHY'S CROCODILE INN
102 Woodfern Road, Neshanic Station

Murphy's Crocodile Inn is situated on a site with a long and colorful history. A train depot once stood here and a hotel was erected in the 1880s. In 1910, a creamery exploded and the flames devoured much of the town including the guesthouse.

The present structure also has an ample and varied story. The building's incarnations include a gas station, barber shop, butcher shop, general store, and finally the present bar and restaurant with top floor apartments.

Strange and inexplicable events have transpired at the eatery. Down in the basement, where the lights regularly turn on by themselves, employees perceive a vague shade prowling in the gloom.

The most terrifying happening took place in the wee hours of the morning as a worker was cleaning up the club. While mopping the floor he noticed large footprints appearing in the wet areas - the treads measured about 3 to 4 feet apart. Utterly fascinated, he kept swabbing and watching and saw a boot materialize and then the entire torso of a gray man in uniform, hat, and a backpack. The worker vaulted to the other side of the room, shaking in his own boots, but continued to watch as the ghost walked *through the wall!*

31

EVERT VAN WICKLE HOUSE
1289 Easton Avenue, Somerset

This beautiful colonial home known as "The Meadows" was built as a wedding gift in 1752 for Evert and Cornelia Van Wickle.

Just five years after they were married, the couple died on the same day, March 3, 1757. They were the first to be buried on the property. A cemetery for the Revolutionary War dead was established on the grounds twenty years later.

In 1976, the last private owner sold the secluded *Meadows* to Franklin Township who maintains the estate as a historic site. The house is meticulously restored and noticeably haunted.

The many documented sightings describe the friendly ghosts as *"playful, pesky and peevish."*

When privately owned, some of the odd happenings experienced by the residents were doilies flying across the room, doors seemed to have a mind of their own, and radios blasted at random day and night.

The owner's dog and cat would sit for hours and stare at the ceiling. What did they perceive that no human eyes could? At times the dog would wag its tail - the cat's reaction was to hiss.

Once a puddle was found on the seat of a chair where only moments before someone had been sitting. The source of the water could not be detected.

Other owners put up with blood curdling screams and icy touches; items disappeared and would later show up in a different part of the house.

One night the sound of an invisible someone was angrily washing dishes, slamming the pots and pans and making quite a racket, *but no body was in the kitchen.*

Incessant knocking was often heard at the front door, but guess what, when the door was answered, *no one was there.*

Out of frustration the man of the house threatened the entities with *"burning down the house"* if they didn't curtail their antics. Shortly thereafter, five apparitions presented themselves in his bedroom. Did they appear to ask for forgiveness? After lingering for a few moments, they floated into the bathroom together and were gone instantly like a puff of smoke.

The irony to the fiery threat is that when the graves of Evert and Cornelia were laid open, only ashes were found. Since cremation was prohibited at the time of their death, the supposition made was that they perished in a fire.

The ghosts who emerged are believed to be the young couple. The names and lives of the others have been forgotten, but their spirits remain reluctant to leave their mortal home.

Who's the ghost who waves to passersby from the Metlar-Bodine House?

METLAR-BODINE HOUSE MUSEUM
River Road, Piscataway

Piscataway was originally settled in 1666 and the Metlar-Bodine House is one of three original dwellings. The historic house operates as a museum presenting state and local history.

When the building was renovated in 1993, the repairs seemed to have revived a ghostly revenant, presumably its former owner, John Metlar.

So many witnesses reported apparitions and mysterious phenomena that the house and its strange goings-on were featured on *The Today Show*. Museum members spotted a man sporting a black bowler hat walk down the hallway and vanish. The house's caretaker heard someone in the attic humming ancient sea ballads. Even passersby report that sometimes an old man waves at them from an upstairs window *when no body is in the building*.

The Bodine Room particularly resonates with supernatural activity. Sensitives detect the aroma of pipe tobacco emanating from a headstone displayed in a corner. Once when the curator was alone, a photograph of Metlar's next-door-neighbor flew off the mantle and across the room. Metlar didn't like the guy when he was alive and must feel compelled to continue to show his dislike from beyond the grave.

ALLEN HOUSE
Metuchen

Of all the colonial buildings still standing in this town, the 1740 Allen House is the oldest and known by its Revolutionary name when it operated as a tavern.

The town suffered many conflicts between British and American troops. History records *carts* of dead bodies in the area after a June 26, 1777 battle around "Oak Tree," the 18th century name for Metuchen. According to old maps, the Allen house stands on property where many skirmishes took place. Most likely the injured were taken to the inn for immediate medical care.

Psychic mediums allege that spirits from several time periods inhabit the house.

The apparition of a man who committed suicide in the house in the 1800s appears to be hanging *between floors*. The former owner confirmed that indeed there had been a floor between the present two stories but that annexation had been removed when the house was restored to its original design.

Mrs. Allen's specter, the innkeeper's wife, stays behind to search for her ten-year-old son who was abducted by Native Americans. Psychic helpers cannot assuage her anguish.

There is no earthly explanation for the peculiar noises heard all over the house. Urgent and persistent banging was heard at the front door one winter's day, but when the owner answered, *no one was there.* Even though the ground was covered with newly fallen snow, *there were no footprints.*

A local historian who resided in the house claimed to have plainly seen the ghost of a Revolutionary soldier walk through the house about a foot off the ground. A cloudy male figure frequented the bedroom, but when he was spoken to, he faded away.

Others swear they've encountered a male phantom with a "distinctive" nose clad in a tan coat and black pants.

A shade who identified herself to a medium as "Mathilda" wears a striped dress and a wedding ring. The medium received the impression of the woman pointing to a deep gash in the band on her finger and exhibiting extreme distress. Why is her spirit so upset about the marred ring?

Animals are known to possess extraordinary senses and the dogs who lived in the Allen House have leapt into bed with their owners from time to time because they have been so frightened by the sights shrouded to the human eye.

The Spy House – home to an amazing array of ghosts.

SPY HOUSE
119 Port Monmouth Road, Port Monmouth

US News & World Report names the 1663 Spy House *"one of the three most haunted houses in America."* Situated behind the sand dunes of Sandy Hook Bay it is the oldest house on the Jersey Shore.

Today the Shoal Harbor Museum is the preferred moniker for the historic jewel, but for some thirty years the building was known simply as the *Spy House.* Visionary Gertrude Neidlinger saved the significant dwelling from the wrecking ball, founded the museum, and functioned as its curator.

During colonial days the British thought that someone in the house was spying on their naval operations. The real spy however peered from nearby Garrett's Hill. The house survived the Revolution by operating as an inn. When the British left their ships to eat at the tavern, the colonists successfully plundered their undermanned vessels by sneaking up to the ships in whaleboats.

Since the 1950s, reports of revenants at the site are rampant. Over thirty ghosts have been counted and over seventy sightings documented.

According to a township employee, the ghosts include, *"Abigail and Peter, Lydia and Reverend Wilson, Captain Morgan, Robert…"*

Loud sobs emanate from a bedroom where Abigail stares out the window looking for her husband who was lost at sea. Ms. Neidlinger felt it was Abigail's son Peter who randomly switched on tape recorders throughout the house that explain its history.

Psychics have perceived Reverend William Wilson, a former owner of the house, perform a funeral service in front of a bedroom fireplace. They have also sensed men strategizing in front of the first floor fireplace.

In his epic tome *GHOSTS, True Encounters with the Great Beyond,* Hans Holzer relates that on July 4, 1975 a group of local boys were in the blue and white bedroom upstairs when all of a sudden the sewing machine door opened by itself and the foot pedals starting pumping without benefit of human feet!

One evening as a volunteer left the building, he witnessed children playing on the grounds. He watched for a few moments and realized there was something unusual about their clothing. Their outfits were of an earlier era; they were wearing provincial garb *and they were ghosts!*

Some people sit for hours in the parking lot waiting for a phantom to put in an appearance.

Thomas Whitlock, the first permanent white resident of New Jersey, built the house. His spirit, on a few occasions, has tagged along with visitors and gone home with them. An employee shared that Thomas likes attention and once she inadvertently brought him home with her. *"He drove my dog crazy."*

From time to time, the aroma of Whitlock's pipe tobacco fills the air. He may also be the culprit who steals workers cigarette packs. *"He always puts them back though."*

At one time pirates commandeered the house. Captain Morgan was a bloodthirsty and brutal buccaneer who despoiled women and murdered children. Youngsters visiting the museum have seen his faceless phantom dressed in a long, dark hooded robe at the top of the stairs and his scary bearded reflection in an upstairs mirror.

During one of the many séances conducted at the house, psychic Jane Doherty contacted a spirit named Robert who claimed to be Captain Morgan's First Mate. Robert revealed the existence of hidden tunnels leading from the house to the harbor. Sonar readings substantiated the possibility of tunnels.

Her psychic impression revealed the presence of a trapdoor used during the Revolution by George Washington when he frequented the inn. Indeed a trapdoor was discovered right where the psychic predicted. History substantiates that Washington stayed at a church in South Amboy, just across the bay.

Approaching the house, a visitor slammed on his brakes - he was certain he had run over a little girl. Fortunately she was only an apparition. Historic records reveal however that a little girl who lived in a nearby house had been run over by a horse and wagon on her way to play at the Spy House.

On stormy autumn nights, an 18th century tragedy replays itself in front of the Cranbury Inn.

CRANBURY INN
21 South Main Street, Cranbury

Cranbury is one of New Jersey's oldest towns and her Main Street was an important stop on the stagecoach route between New York and Philadelphia. Before that, the thoroughfare was a Native American trail. Legend states that numerous human and animal spirits still haunt the historic roadway.

One spook in particular is Philadelphia merchant William Christie who on October 14, 1796, fell to his death from a stagecoach in front of the Cranbury Inn. The Scottish native was buried across the street in the First Presbyterian Church graveyard where his tombstone can be observed.

Locals claim that on stormy October nights the tragedy is re-enacted. Residents swear they hear the clamor of the horses' whinny, the crunch of stagecoach wheels, and the young man's screams.

A ghost who has taken up residence inside the Cranbury Inn uses the ladies restroom. When an employee entered the lounge she encountered a vaporous form opening a stall door.

The South Jersey Ghost Research organization has captured the spirits on film in the form of orbs dashing about the basement and dining areas.

Burlington County Prison is a hotbed of supernatural activity.

BURLINGTON COUNTY PRISON
128 High Street, Mount Holly

The word "PRISON" is chiseled in the thick gray stone, skeleton keys surrounded by chains adorn each side of the entryway and black iron bars cover the windows of the 1810 stronghold. Though the cells are empty a lingering presence remains.

The jail's architect, Robert Mills, also designed the Washington Monument. Mills planned a "progressive" prison layout - individual cells were thought more suitable by the reformist movement popular in the early 19th century.

This was the country's oldest operating prison in existence until it closed its heavy oak paneled doors in 1965. The building has since been restored to its original appearance and now operates as a museum.

In 1999, the historic slammer opened its doors to a brigade of New Jersey ghost hunters led by paranormal investigator Dave Juliano. The photos Juliano snapped in the prison that night reveal orbs of light, misty vapors, and "ectoplasm," all evidence of a ghostly presence. Juliano captured chilling voices on tape - Electronic Voice Phenomena (EVP) - entreating *"help me, help me."* He also observed the apparition of a man walk down the hall and into a cell.

Some feel the phantom is Joseph Clough who was convicted of murder for beating his mistress to death with a table leg. Clough was shackled by leg irons to a bolt in the floor of Cell 5 for many months before he was finally hanged in the 1850s.

The haunting at the prison started soon after Clough's execution. Sounds of heavy chains and incessant moaning began to be heard. Former inmates claimed to see cigarettes floating in mid-air and several guards reported sensing a presence in the cell when no one was physically there.

Psychic investigator Hildred Robinette, who has seen ghosts all her life, witnessed three male ghosts in the prison's basement. One even told her his name – Andrew Morrison. In the death row cell she saw a man crouching in the corner. He turned to her and angrily hissed, *"What are you looking at?"* When the wraith started flinging curses at her she fled the cubicle.

It's no surprise that vestiges of the past still linger at the county jail. Men imprisoned here carried a lot of hatred and anger and many were routinely executed in the back yard. Their anguish is still palpable.

A *New York Times* reporter who covered the ghost hunters' investigation observed something strange. An antique prison cot that had been leaning against the wall was found lying down on the floor as if someone unseen was getting ready to sleep on it.

At that point all the visitors left, for the hour had come for those doing time in the afterlife to bed down.

THE HOUSE on 5TH STREET
Camden

Number 522 - 5th Street, a gray stone residence with a nice backyard, no longer exits. The modest house was built during Prohibition when Camden was a sought after place to live. The interior room design was practical and arranged in the "railroad flats" manner; this meant you had to walk through several rooms to get from one end of the house to another.

The most stunning feature of the house was a curved staircase with a beautifully carved wooden railing. During the Martin's family stay in the house, the banister's patina glowed and seemed to illuminate the stairway.

The family learned to live with their invisible co-habitants in the sixty-year-old house. The most frequent anomalie they experienced was the sound of rustling skirts.

The middle bedroom was the epicenter of paranormal events. All alone in the house, one daughter once heard someone come up the stairs and enter this room. The invisible wraith sighed as if in great sadness. When she peered into the room, the bed springs squeaked as if someone had lain down.

Another night she undressed in the dark and placed her clothing on the bed. When she did so, someone sighed and rolled over. Thinking it was her cousin, she moved the clothes to a nearby chair. At breakfast she asked her mother where her cousin was. Her mom had no idea – she hadn't seen her in weeks! *Who was it in the bed that night?*

The ghost's identity remained shrouded in mystery until shortly before the family moved out of their haunted dwelling. A psychic medium made a visit to 522 - 5th Street and immediately received an impression of a woman and a little boy. The psychic ascertained the woman's name and perceived that she had fallen down the stairs to her death. Research authenticated the intuited name was indeed that of a previous owner.

One of the most terrifying experiences happened in the basement. A family friend was going through the trunks left behind by a prior resident. As she riffled through the clothes looking for a vintage dress to wear to a dance, she was certain someone was watching her.

The atmosphere was electric and her hair stood on end, literally, she touched her locks and they were sticking straight up! Mustering all her courage she turned around slowly...a gray mist swirled and gradually formed into a human shape. The head was most prominent and the eyeholes were empty sockets.

Gasping for breath the girl actually crawled on all fours up the stairs and out into the fresh air.

The ghosts continued to haunt the dwelling for nearly thirty years until the structure was torn down.

GABREIL DAVEIS TAVERN
4th Avenue, Glendora

Built in the Georgian style, the 1756 colonial tavern is one of New Jersey's oldest historical landmarks.

In earlier days, the Gloucester County tavern served as an inn for boatmen who transported their products to Philadelphia via Big Timber Creek. The house was akin to today's town hall. The old rafters seem to retain the vibrations of the spirited discussions and local elections held here.

The brick and stone building was also used as a hospital during the American Revolution. Wounded soldiers sought treatment in the attic. Some rested to recover – some never did – and they remain here in a perpetual state of *un*rest. Although their names are forgotten, their presence fills the upper room with a sickeningly feeling; their eerie bloodstains still show on the floorboards. If you listen closely the sounds of tormented men suffering the wounds of war audibly drift through the air.

Photos taken in the house show orbs of light prevalent in the attic suggesting a ghostly presence.

Specters sighted in the woods out back turn and flee as if they suspect they're encroaching on unfriendly turf. Could these skulking shades be one-time spies?

A visit to the tavern is a step back in time, and perhaps, into another realm.

Legend says a Tory spy was hung inside the 1762 Seven Stars Tavern.

SEVEN STARS TAVERN
Woodstown

Today, this handsome 1762 farmhouse in Pilesgrove Township is a beautifully restored private home.

When the residence operated as a tavern, it may well have been the first drive-in in the country. A small window off the taproom was set up so that riders could quaff their drinks without dismounting their horse.

At one time, however, the home was heralded as the most haunted house in New Jersey.

During the 1800s the site was a working farm and the help bunked in the attic. The upstairs room was a hotbed of paranormal activity. Disembodied footsteps were regularly heard climbing the stairs. Restless spirits wrangled in the hall shoving and pushing each other.

In the 1930s, farm workers had the encounter of a lifetime. The apparition of a man hanging from an attic beam manifested before their eyes. Gruesome gurgling noises issued from the specter and bloody foam oozed from his mouth. The bug-eyed phantom was wild with pain and frantically pointed to the noose around his neck plainly urging them to remove the ligature.

The workers were riveted and unable to move until the vision faded away.

OLD LAWSON PLACE
Vincentown

In the dead of night a light glowed in the attic of the weathered clapboard house known as the "Old Lawson Place." At times, horrific screams issued from the building disturbing the still air - and all who heard the awful shrieks.

Alta Cossart Lawson was the cause of the commotion in more ways than one. She began her reign of terror by wresting control of the Lawson Iron Foundry away from her compliant husband. Her brash demeanor and lavish spending bankrupt the business and ruined their marriage.

When the company folded and Lawson passed, Alta, their son Lambert, and his wife Sophia lived together in the deteriorating house. Alta subverted her son's marriage, secretly enabling his drinking.

One night in 1890 the tension in the debilitated household was at an all time high. It was Alta who goaded her inebriated son into attacking Sophia with an ax. Sophia tried to escape from the house but Lambert severed her from behind and her head rolled down the steps and into the front yard.

Lambert was committed to an insane asylum. Alta stayed on at the house - even after death. Clad in a purple silk dress, her ghost haunted the ravaged home and the streets surrounding it.

NAVAL AIR WARFARE CENTER
Lakehurst

Although the Lakehurst Navy Base has an eighty five-year history, it is most remembered as the site of the *Hindenburg* tragedy.

On May 6, 1937, thirty-six individuals lost their lives in the fiery crash. It is said that the remains of some of those who perished were buried here and many believe the victims' spirits still haunt the location.

At the time of the tragedy, the Branch Medical Clinic operated as a hospital and morgue for the *Hindenburg's* casualties. No one dreams of sleeping in the building's basement even though comfortable accommodations are provided for the staff on guard duty. And for good reason.

A chief making his rounds one night pulled on a doorknob to make sure it was secure. When he walked away, the doorknob rattled back at him. He noticed lights on in the upper floors when there was no one else in the building that could have turned them on.

At times, clinic workers feel certain they are being watched. Once a young petty officer had the fright of his life when he turned around to see who was there. He glimpsed a silver-haired woman in a white gown floating in the air - her face was obscured.

The clinic is not the only spooky spot.

An airman clad in vintage fly gear has greeted workers in Hangar One with a hearty *"Good morning!"* When they do a double take, the flyboy is gone.

Some evenings muffled undertones of men shouting *"Away the lines, away the lines!"* and *"She's afire!"* echo on the tarmac near the historic hangar.

Historic Hangar One - site of the Hindenburg disaster.

GARDEN STATE PARKWAY
Toms River

For years the story has been told of the Parkway Phantom haunting a short stretch of the highway in Toms River.

The tall male ghost is always described as wearing a long, belted raincoat. Typically observed on foggy nights, he waves his arms wildly as if he wants to cross the roadway.

Motorists have stopped to help the man, but when they do he's nowhere in sight.

Others feel his erratic behavior is a deliberate warning signal to motorists to slow down and be careful of danger ahead. Perhaps he was a casualty himself and wants to keep others out of harm's way.

The strangest thing is the way the apparition abnormally bends his arms from the elbow moving both at the same time.

The sightings date back to 1955 when the Garden State Parkway was first completed. The state police will not comment on the reports but they do admit to a larger than usual number of accidents in the area.

Most sightings take place along an eight-mile length of roadway near Exit 82 in the vicinity of the Toms River Barracks of the New Jersey State Police.

MANSION OF HEALTH
Long Beach Island

Today the Surf City Hotel sits on the site formerly occupied by the 1822 Mansion of Health. For years the three-towered structure was the shore's grandest hotel and the island's most haunted building.

One of New Jersey's most savage storms hit on April 18, 1854. The wooden schooner *Powhatan* had left Rotterdam and was drawing near her New York destination. On board the packet ship were three hundred affluent German immigrants on their way to America and a new life.

A springtime crossing of the turbulent North Atlantic can be treacherous so Captain Myers was relieved when he saw the land birds that signaled the schooner was approaching the coast.

Fate, however, was a cruel mistress that day. The weather changed quickly and the ship was caught in an onslaught of strong winds and huge waves. Stormy seas raged and the *Powhatan* found herself struggling to stay afloat in the full-fledged blizzard. The foundering ship was vanquishing in the violent shoals. Lifesavers on shore were helpless and the situation for the *Powhatan*, hopeless.

At the time, Edward Jennings was the Mansion of Health's caretaker and a designated wreckmaster responsible for reporting any shipwrecks in his area.

The corpses from the schooner washed ashore. The sight was awful - mothers clutched babies in their arms; couples embraced each other for the last time.

Jennings went about his work piling *Powhatan's* cadavers on the sand. The coroner inquired if any valuables had been found. *"Not a thing,"* Jennings tersely replied. The victims were buried in a mass grave in Manahawkin.

Some months later two men found a huge pile of leather money belts that had been cut open and secreted away near the Mansion; a recent storm had washed the sand away from the hiding place.

Although he was not formally charged with the theft, Jennings' reputation was ruined. He left New Jersey and headed South. When word got back that Jennings had been murdered in a barroom brawl, many believed that justice had finally been served.

The Old Mansion's clientele discovered more fashionable digs, but phantom visitors found the accommodations much to their liking. For years the apparition of a woman holding a young child in her arms was frequently seen standing at the window.

Inevitably, the forsaken hotel burned to the ground. The building may be gone, but they say the screams and cries of the doomed ship's passengers and crew can still be heard on Surf City's sands.

Mournful sobs fill the Atlantic County Courthouse.

ATLANTIC COUNTY COURTHOUSE
5909 Main Street, Mays Landing

Workers at the county courthouse have certainly had their share of experiences with the paranormal. Ghostly sobs fill the 1887 courtroom, the halls of justice jingle with the sound of clanking keys, and elevators, lights and water faucets seem to have a mind of their own.

Who or what is causing these disturbances? One possible explanation is that executions used to take place in the 19th century at the "hanging tree" planted outside the courthouse. Do the spirits of those lynched on the property still linger there? Or is it their loved ones grieving over the verdict?

Some feel the perpetrator could be the man who hung himself in the bell tower or maybe it's the jail inmate, who while assigned to clean the building, tried to break into the safe in one of the offices. He died of a heart attack before he could get it open.

Poltergeist activity is also prevalent. In the break room an officer observed a soap detergent bottle fall over and a soup ladle fly from the table and land in front of the microwave oven. The dish it was in flipped upside down right before his eyes.

"It is definitely haunted. There are no two ways about it," said the president of the county historical society.

The Winterwood Gift Shoppe harbors the spirits of the Hildreth sisters.

WINTERWOOD GIFT SHOPPE
3137 Route 9 South, Rio Grande

This place is so haunted a sign hangs outside notifying all who enter of the unseen specters lurking within.

The Hildreth family was one of the founding families of Cape May. Joshua Hildreth built the house, now the Winterwood Gift Shoppe, in 1722. The last descendants to live there were two spinster sisters, Hester and Lucille, who died in 1948 and 1954 respectively. Inseparable when alive, they remain together in the afterlife at their ancestral home. Their soft voices and footsteps infiltrate the house and their shadowy forms have been discerned inside and out.

A white robed phantom likes to glide from the house and across the lawn to the family burial ground out back. As she reaches her destination, she vanishes.

The Hildreth's housed a colonial soldier and in gratitude he carved the beautiful mantle showcased in the shop. His spirit pervades the space as well.

Other anomalies include merchandise disappearing and reappearing, unexplainable noises and most mystifying, employees watch in wonder as store displays dismantle before their eyes.

Visit this lovely boutique and a misty form floating in the doorway might greet you. Amusing or terrifying? Only you can decide.

CAPE MAY

The oldest seaside resort in the United States is New Jersey's most haunted city. Cape May, a designated national historic landmark, is an actual museum of Victorian architecture. Over 600 vintage wooden structures, dating from 1800 to 1910, ornament an area of less than two square miles.

Whalers first settled the area in the early 1600s and the area was known as a resort long before the Revolutionary War. Steamship travel from Philadelphia and train service in 1830, shaped Cape May into a fashionable and popular destination.

Once known as the "playground of presidents," Abraham Lincoln lodged at the Mansion House in 1849, Franklin Pierce visited in 1855, James Buchanan vacationed here in 1858, Ulysses S. Grant in 1873, and Chester A. Arthur stayed in 1893.

Today, thousands of tourists crowd the tangled streets each year, sharing their space with illusions of earlier days. Filmy figures have been sighted strolling along Congress Street, fishermen and visitors encounter eerie spirits along the coast and at Cape May Lighthouse. On Jackson Street, where the devastating fire of 1836 consumed dozens of dwellings, denizens arrive at dawn and appear to be looking for their loved ones displaced during the fiery confusion.

Fully one-third of the state's ghostly population resides in the Victorian enclave, which forces the question "why is Cape May so haunted?"

Charles J. Adams III and David J. Seibold, authors of two books devoted to the city's ghosts, have a theory. They say that since the human body consists of a certain amount of electrical energy, at times of extreme stress or trauma, this human electricity is discharged from the body, released into the atmosphere, and lodges itself in other physical structures such as furniture and walls. The authors go on to say that gifted psychics can therefore "read" the room, or the object (a process known as psychometry), and provide us with glimpses into the past. Likewise, refurbishment in the old buildings wakes up the sleeping energy, or spirits if you will, and that is what causes the dead to come to life

Paranormal researcher Al Rauber originated the "Haunted Cape May Tour." He has captured ghostly voices on tape and asserts that the moisture-laden atmosphere is the medium by which the abstract energy manifests.

Reason number three - surrounded by such charm and beauty, why would anyone, dead or alive, want to leave Cape May?

The following images are a photographic mini-tour of some of Cape May's most haunted places.

The EMLEN PHYSICK ESTATE, 1048 Washington Street, houses the Mid-Atlantic Center for the Arts, and the spirit of its former owner, Dr. Emlen Physick Jr., whom they suspect has never left.

At the WASHINGTON INN, 801 Washington Street, a spirit christened "Elizabeth" sends shivers down the spine of employees as she softly calls them by name.

THE SOUTHERN MANSION, 720 Washington Street, lodges the specter of Esther, the niece of the man who built the 1863 Italianate masterpiece. Guests have reported seeing her reflection in mirrors and smelling her perfume.

The INN at 22 JACKSON has a permanent guest named Esmerelda.
She died in the turret room and now haunts it. Esmerelda is a gentle,
comforting spirit who loves children.

67

A temperamental Irish maid haunts the Edwardian WINDWARD HOUSE INN at 24 Jackson Street. Her friendly spirit brazenly sits on the bed in the Wicker Room.

68

*In a photograph taken on the staircase at THE SEA HOLLY INN,
815 Stockton Avenue, the ghostly image of a woman in Victorian dress
developed. Ghostly figures are sighted in bedrooms and halls in this
"enchanted" B&B.*

The ANGEL OF THE SEA, 7 Trenton Avenue, houses at least three ghosts. The spirit of a teen-age girl who fell to her death from an upper floor ledge, a soldier who died of tuberculosis on the premises, and the daughter of a former owner.

70

HIGBEE BEACH
Cape May Point

Higbee Beach is an isolated spot located on the Delaware side of Cape May Point. Popular with sunbathers, fishermen, and bird watchers, the area is a controlled habitat for migratory songbirds, raptors, and butterflies.

The tangled terrain and eerie cries of unseen animals and birds secreting themselves in the marshy pools and swampland echo in the ether along this desolate stretch of bayshore beach. What a perfect setting for a haunting...

A long held legend is that phantom pirates still guard their treasure buried on the beach long ago.

Another oft-told tale is that the protected sand dunes are the stomping ground of former plantation owner Old Man Higbee. The story goes that Higbee was buried face down so that he could meet Satan face to face. Sometimes in the early morning hours, his pale gray luminous ghost is seen gliding over the dunes and into the surf.

An additional soul stuck between dimensions is said to be Higbee's personal slave. Charged in life to keep watch over his master's grave, he continues his vigil to this very day.

71

BIBLIOGRAPHY

Adams, Charles J. III, *Cape May Ghost Stories, Book Two.*
Exeter House Books, Reading, PA; 1996.

Bertrand, Bruce, "The Ghost at Darress Theatre in Boonton."
Weird NJ, Bloomfield, NJ; Volume #13, October 1999.

Hauck, Dennis William, *Haunted Places: The National Directory.*
Penguin Books, New York, NY; 1996.

Holzer, Hans, *GHOSTS: True Encounters with the Great Beyond.*
Levanthal Press, Conway, NH; 1998.

Johnston, Eileen Luz, *Phyllis – The Library Ghost?.* Johnston
Letter Co., Inc., Newark, NJ; 1991.

Lloyd, John Bailey, *Six Miles at Sea: A Pictorial History of Long
Beach Island, NJ.* Down Shore Publishing, Tuckerton, NJ; 1985.

Mittelbach, Margaret and Crewdson, Michael, *"In Pursuit of Spirits
Doing Time in the Afterlife."* The New York Times, New York,
NY; October 29, 1999.

Moran, Gwendolyn, "Ghastly Ghost Stories, " *Yesterday/Today in
New Jersey*, Newark, NJ; Oct/Nov 1995.

Moran, Mark, "The Wallet Man of Morristown." *Weird NJ*,
Bloomfield, NJ; Volume #9, October 1997.

Myers, Arthur, *The Ghostly Register.* Contemporary Books,
Chicago, IL; 1986.

Reynolds, James, *Ghosts in American Houses.* Paperback Library,
New York, NY; 1950.

Rose, Elaine, "Courting Ghosts?" *The Atlantic City Press*, Atlantic
City, NJ; October 31, 1992.

Sceurman, Mark and Moran, Mark, "The Ghosts of the Union
Hotel." *Weird NJ*, Bloomfield, NJ; Volume #8, May 1997.

_____, "Ghosts of New Jersey." *Weird NJ*, Bloomfield, NJ:
Volume #9, October 1997.

_____, *"Weird NJ* Helps Choose Location for Tim Burton Shoot." *Weird NJ*, Bloomfield, NJ; Vol. #11, October 1998.

_____, "Mixing with the Spirits in Neshanic Station." *Weird NJ*, Bloomfield, NJ; Volume #15, October 2000.

Siebold, Daniel and Adams, Charles J. III, *Legends of Long Beach Island.* Exeter House Books, Reading, Pa; 1985.

_____, *Cape May Ghost Stories.* Exeter House Books, Reading PA & Barnegat Light, NJ, 1988.

Westergaard, Barbara, *New Jersey A Guide To The State*, Second Edition. Rutgers University Press, New Brunswick, NJ; 1998.

Zayas, David, "The White Lady of Branch Brook Park." *Weird NJ*, Bloomfield, NJ; Volume #12, May 1999.

Zeman, Mary Beth, "The History and Mystery of Hobart Manor." *WP: The Magazine of William Paterson University*, Wayne, NJ; Fall/Winter 1999.

Additionally, the following websites were referenced:

Flemington, NJ: http://www.flemington.net
Gloucester Township: http://www.glotwp.com/history
Haunted New Jersey: http://www.hauntednewjersey.com
Liberty State Park: http://www.libertystatepark.com
New Jersey Ghost Hunters Society: http://www.njghs.net
New Jersey's Ghosts and Hauntings: http://www.ghostpage.com
The New York Times: http://www.nytimes.com
The Press of Atlantic City: http://www.pressplus.com
Psychic Jane Doherty: http://www.janedoherty.com
Real Haunted Houses: http://www.realhaunts.com
Ringwood Manor: http://www.ringwoodmanor.com
The Shadowlands: http://www.shadowlands.com
South Jersey Ghost Research Organization: http://www.sjgr.org